GREAT DISASTERS in HISTORY

Betty Lou Kratoville

Copyright ©1994 by High Noon Books. All rights reserved. Printed in the United States of America. Users are permitted to copy pages in this book for classroom use as long as they are not sold.

High Noon Books
20 Commercial Boulevard
Novato, CA 94949-6191

International Standard Book Number: 0-87879-975-3

4 3 2 1 0 9 8 7 6 5
1 0 9 8 7 6 5 4 3 2

Contents

INTRODUCTION iv

The Black Plague 5

The Johnstown Flood 10

The Great Galveston Gale 15

Panic at the Iroquois Theater 20

Double Disaster in San Francisco 25

Sinking of the Titanic 30

Final Flight of the Hindenburg 35

Fire Storm at the Circus 40

The World Blows Up at Texas City 45

Eruption at Mount St. Helens 50

Challenger — Tragedy in the Sky 55

The Chernobyl Catastrophe 60

VOCABULARY 67

Introduction

What is it about disasters that is so fascinating? A highway accident, for example, may cause traffic to back up for miles simply because many drivers slow down to peer at the scene. Do these people scrutinize an accident because they want to see the gory details — or is it because it gives them a feeling of well-being? After all, they are intact, their car is in one undented piece, and they are on their way to wherever they were going. It's a safe, comfortable, secure feeling, and they cannot in all truth be faulted for it.

The same is true of major natural or man-made disasters. We sit before our television sets, warm and dry, and are horrified by some of the events the camera is witnessing for us. We are truly shocked, truly sympathetic at the plight of the characters in this real-life drama. Yet we are able to get up from our chairs, flick off the television set, and go in for our evening meal without a second thought for the tragedy we have just witnessed. "There but for the grace of God go I," seems often to be the prevailing attitude.

The disasters in this book begin with the Black Plague in 1347-1351 and end with the nuclear catastrophe at Chernobyl in 1986. The author's most difficult task was to select 12 disasters out of hundreds. A mere mention of a book on disasters prompted unsolicited suggestions. Everyone seemed to have a favorite disaster, and no two were alike. A decision was ultimately made to opt for *variety*, and so the following events in addition to the plague and nuclear explosion are included: a theater fire, a volcano eruption, a dirigible crash, a capsized ship, a circus holocaust, an earthquake, a hurricane, a flood, and the deaths of a town and a spaceship.

What do these events have in common? Several things. First of all, their very suddenness. At one moment the lives of the people involved were serene, even joyful. The next moment their world was split apart, and the thought uppermost in their minds was survival, pure and simple. Secondly, many facets of the human conditions emerged — people were courageous and cowardly, selfish and unselfish, calm and panicky, worried and relieved. There are heroes and heroines, villains and villainesses. It does give one pause — "How would I act in a similar situation?" In truth, one does not really know the answer to that question — and probably does not really wish to know.

A sense of history will be gained from reading about the twelve disasters and completing the exercises that follow each one. However, for one to fully comprehend these legendary events, it is important that the vocabulary of each one is studied and mastered in advance. Difficult words have been underlined and should be looked up in the vocabulary section (beginning on page 67) and thoroughly discussed before any script is read for the first time. It is recommended that vocabulary words be used in an oral discussion so that pronunciation and meaning become clear.

The Black Plague

The date was: Approximately 1347 to 1351

The place was: Europe

Background

Courtesy: The British Museum

The Black Plague! The worst natural disaster mankind has ever suffered. How did it start? No one knows for sure. But all are agreed that the blame should be squarely placed on that evil-looking animal — the black rat. It was, in fact, a very simple sequence. The rats carried the plague germ in their bloodstream. Fleas sucked the blood of the infected rats. Then they moved on to human beings. In the 14th century rats were common; baths and clean living conditions were not. Homes and clothing were full of fleas. No one gave a second thought to a little flea bite. The poor people had other things to worry about, such as getting enough to eat!

We know now that the Black Plague took three forms. The best known of these is called the bubonic plague. The victim has a very high fever, chills, and painful swellings in the armpits and groin. In bubonic plague, death comes within a week. In another form of the plague, the germs enter the victim's bloodstream. Then death can occur quickly — even overnight! In the third form, the germs enter the lungs. Once again death takes place in just a few days.

The Disaster

In 1347 twelve ships landed in Sicily, an island off the coast of Italy. Some of the people on the ships had plague. In just a few days, the Sicilians began to grow sick. They quickly made the twelve ships leave but it was too late.

A year later three ships docked at Genoa, Italy. They had come from Caffa, a port on the Black Sea, where many citizens had fallen ill. The ships probably held rats that carried plague. They also had sailors and passengers on board who were already infected with plague.

And then there were the trade routes. Trade between Europe and the East was lively. It is possible, therefore, that the plague also entered Europe as traders traveled from one place to another.

The plague had struck in full force! The countries of Europe were all but wiped out. In France people in both the cities and the countryside grew sick and died. Reports from French travelers were terrifying. They found cattle wandering around with no one to take care of them. Houses and barns were empty. Whole populations of towns and villages were totally wiped out.

It was in 1348 that the plague somehow reached across the English Channel to England. Here so many died, there were not enough workmen to bring in the crops. Food prices soared, adding to the general misery.

The plague overtook the people of Vienna about a year later in the summer of 1349. So many grew ill, there were not enough well citizens to give the dead a decent burial. The corpses were carried out of the city to deep pits that were quickly filled with bodies.

One <u>incident</u> was downright creepy! A ship carrying wool left London. By the time it ran aground on the coast of Norway, most of the crew had died. It was practically a ghost ship. And so the plague came to the Scandinavian countries. It spared no one there. Even the half brothers of the King of Sweden died.

In fact, the plague did not spare royal persons. Among those who died were the wife of the King of Aragon, the King of Castile, the daughter of the King of England, the Queen of Burgundy, the Queen of Navarre, two Archbishops of Canterbury, and the Patriarch Archbishop of Catania in Italy.

What were Europeans doing to fight the plague? A number of things. Some doctors fled; others tried to treat the sick and dying. There were medical men who thought diet might be a cause and ruled out certain foods. Others thought that smoke from fires would prevent the plague. Some doctors felt that staying cheerful was the answer. Then there were the quacks who sold the people charms and potions to protect against the plague. Nothing did any good. People died with or without the care of a doctor. And, of course, the doctors and the quacks died, too.

Some Europeans turned to religion during these terrible years. They felt that the plague was God's punishment for their sins. As death drew near, they called for their priests. They sought forgiveness for their sins so they would be sure to get into heaven. However, many of the priests had fled. Those who were brave enough to remain to comfort the dying often died themselves.

The year 1350 was proclaimed to be a Holy Year. Fifteen thousand people from all over Europe traveled to Rome. They hoped that such a <u>pilgrimage</u> would keep them from getting the plague. It didn't. Instead it helped the disease to spread. About ninety percent of the people who started out on the pilgrimage died. Because the church seemed helpless to stop the plague, religion was greatly weakened during this period.

The Aftermath

Many important historical events resulted from the Black Plague. For example, Greenland had been settled by the Norsemen. They planned to use it as a jumping off place for the settlement of colonies in North America. The plague changed all that. First of all, it reached Greenland and killed many of the people there. Secondly, shipments from Iceland and Scandinavia that were needed to keep the Greenlanders alive were held up by the plague.

Food and other important items did not get through. The settlement died out. It had to be discovered all over again much later. In this way, the plague may have held up settlement of North America for many years.

It may also have been the plague that turned England into an important sheep-raising country. The large landowners could not find enough workers for their farms so they switched to sheep which required many fewer hands.

It seems somewhat strange that the marvelous period known as the <u>Renaissance</u> began just about the time the Black Plague began to lessen. Creativity in art, literature, and music began to <u>flourish</u> as it never had flourished before. Because the plague had greatly weakened the church, men and women stopped thinking so much about life after death. They began to think much more about their lives on earth. The plague was almost over. If one were still alive, it was time to rejoice. It was a time for optimism, for new ideas.

Actually the plague was not over for all time. Minor plagues have continued through the years. In 1893 six million people died from a plague in India. In 1899 South America suffered a plague. But by this time the causes of plague were known. Steps could be taken to limit them. In this century plague has almost disappeared all over the world. Many people in science and medicine are working hard to continue this splendid trend.

On a separate sheet of paper list all the underlined words in the story of the Black Plague. Find them in the vocabulary section beginning on page 67. Review their meaning and pronunciation. Choose any four and write a sentence for each one.

The Black Plague
IN OTHER WORDS

LESSON NO. 1

Here are 12 words that appear in *The Black Plague*. The object of the assignment is to find words of 2, 3, 4, or more letters by using letters from each clue word IN THE SAME ORDER IN WHICH THEY APPEAR IN THE WORD.

Example: d<u>is</u>aster = is   (This goes in the 5 point column.)
di<u>sa</u>s<u>t</u>er = sat   (This goes in the 10 point column.)
di<u>sas</u>t<u>e</u>r = date   (This goes in the 15 point column.)

A perfect score is 360. Remember! You cannot change the order of the letters in the clue word.

Clue Word	5 Points	10 Points	15 Points
disaster	is	sat	date
clothing			
inflicted			
practically			
daughter			
Europeans			
archbishop			
pilgrimage			
Renaissance			
flourished			
population			
forgiveness			
Total Points			

GRAND TOTAL _____

The Black Plague
ACTIVITIES

LESSON NO. 2

In Class

1. In a dictionary look up the words *plague* and *epidemic*. Write the definitions below. Is there a difference between the two? Explain your answer.

   _____
   _____
   _____
   _____

2. There is a plague in the world today. It is known as AIDS. Write at least 3 facts that you know to be true about this terrible disease. Then have a class discussion.

   a. _____
   b. _____
   c. _____

At Home

1. Ask a parent when you received shots as a small child as a prevention against disease. What illnesses were you immunized against? Have you ever had a booster shot? Write all this information down and bring it to class to compare with others.

2. Write a short paragraph about the last time you were given a shot. What was it for? How did it feel?

At the Library

1. At one time smallpox was considered to be a deadly disease. For centuries epidemics of smallpox killed and scarred people all over the world. Today there is no smallpox in the world. Ask the librarian to help you find out how it was eradicated.

2. Do you know what must be done when a person is bitten by a rabid animal? Look it up.

The Johnstown Flood

The date was: May 31, 1889

The place was: Johnstown, Pennsylvania

Background

In the early 1800's travel between the major cities in Pennsylvania was a hardship. It was also difficult to transport goods. Something needed to be done so that people and freight could get from one place to another safely and comfortably. The solution seemed to be a canal between the valley

Courtesy: Pennsylvania Historical Society

town of Johnstown and Pittsburgh 75 miles to the east. Its main purpose would be to handle east and west barge traffic. By the middle of the century such a canal was finished. It had to have a steady supply of water so the South Fork Dam was built about 14 miles upstream from Johnstown. It was an impressive structure, 100 feet high and 272 feet at its base. The flow of water from the huge lake behind the dam was controlled by outlet pipes. There was also a spillway at one end that could carry off 45,000 gallons of water per second.

Only a few years later railroad tracks were laid between Johnstown and Pittsburgh. That put an end to canal traffic since trains were faster and cheaper. From then on the canal and the dam were neglected. Badly needed repairs were not made. The dam, now without any function, grew weaker and weaker.

At this time Johnstown had a population of about 30,000. It was a busy place. Because it was close to coal mines, iron deposits, and limestone quarries, it had grown into a large industrial center. Also, the area around the South Fork Dam had become something of a resort. The fine fishing attracted rich men from Pittsburgh. Many of them built cottages and clubhouses on the waterfront.

The Disaster

The rain began on May 30th. All night long the chilly downpour continued. In those days rainfall was not measured in inches as it is now, so no one knows exactly how much rain fell. But it was enough to cause creeks and rivers to overflow. It was later estimated that during the morning of May 31st the swollen creeks and the heavy rains were pouring up to 75,000 gallons of water per second into the lake behind the dam. In Johnstown water also began to creep slowly up the streets and into buildings. The residents of Johnstown were not alarmed because this sort of thing had happened before. But they surely were not prepared for the terrifying events that followed!

Shortly before noon the lake began to pour over the dam. Three hours later the <u>unthinkable</u> happened — at 3:10 P.M. the dam collapsed. An <u>incredible</u> 25 million tons of water roared down the valley. It created a <u>monstrous</u> wall of water 40 feet high. Every single thing in its path was wiped out. Trees, no matter how large, were uprooted. Farm buildings and <u>fertile</u> fields were washed away.

As it traveled, the wall of water became even more dangerous. It picked up tons of <u>debris</u> as it rushed over the land. It smashed through several tiny towns on its way to Johnstown where the poor people had absolutely no warning. As they peered through the rain, they thought they were seeing a cloud of dust or smoke coming towards them. No one had any idea that what they were really seeing was a solid wall of water full of railroad cars, trees, steel rails, chunks of buildings, bodies of men, women, children, and farm animals. When they finally realized what was happening, everyone ran for his life. For the next ten minutes terrified families lost track of one another as they tried to get out of the way of the deadly torrent rushing towards them. Their frantic efforts were useless. About 1,000 people died in the first rush of the filthy waters.

Things quickly grew worse in Johnstown. A huge jam of debris piled up at a town bridge. Soon it grew to 30 feet in height and extended 30 blocks into the city. No one knows how the fire in the pile of debris started. It may have resulted from a chemical <u>reaction</u> between the contents of a wrecked railroad car loaded with lime and the flood waters. But at sundown a small flicker of flame was spotted by dazed survivors of the flood. Oil from a wrecked railroad tank car had washed into and around the debris. That was all that was needed to turn the small flicker into an <u>inferno</u>. Many people in the pile of wood and steel burned to death while their friends and neighbors stood by helplessly. There was nothing anyone could do.

All in all, more than 2,200 people died in the disaster. And it had lasted less than an hour!

Aftermath

The survivors were in <u>pitiful</u> shape. They had no food, no clothing, and, worst of all, no homes. Many were sick and injured and needed medical help. All were wet and hungry. Children had lost one or both of their parents. Parents had lost children. Husbands sought wives. Wives sought their husbands. Ninety-nine families, some with as many as ten members, were entirely gone. There was worry about the disease and epidemics that often follow such disasters. The poor <u>stricken</u> town needed help. And it needed it fast!

People in Pittsburgh and the nearby areas organized a relief committee at once. Within 24 hours a train loaded with food, clothes, medicine, and other supplies was on its way. It could not get all the way into Johnstown because so much of the railroad track had been washed away. Goods were transferred to wagons for the rest of the journey. About three million dollars (a vast sum of money at that time) was sent by people around the world to help the Johnstown survivors rebuild their lives. Somehow the city recovered although it was not until 1937 after several more floods that a flood control system was built.

Today Johnstown is a thriving city which produces furniture, textiles, and clay products. Most important of all, its people no longer live in fear of flood.

———————————

On a separate sheet of paper list all of the underlined words in the story about the Johnstown Flood. Find them in the vocabulary section beginning on page 67. Review their meaning and pronunciation. Choose any five and write a sentence for each one.

The Johnstown Flood
IDIOMS

LESSON NO. 1

An idiom is a group of words that do not mean exactly what they say. For example, "Hold your horses" means "Wait a minute." Below are 12 underlined idioms. Write their meaning on the line under each one.

After the flood the people of Johnstown

1. were <u>in a jam</u>.

2. knew that it had <u>rained cats and dogs</u>.

3. <u>put up a good front</u>.

4. <u>kept a stiff upper lip</u>.

5. were <u>under the weather</u>.

6. had to <u>face the music</u>.

7. were <u>up the creek without a paddle</u>.

8. had to <u>wipe the slate clean</u>.

9. were going <u>around in circles</u>.

10. were <u>down in the mouth</u>.

11. found their lives were <u>out of whack</u>.

12. were <u>fit to be tied</u>.

The Johnstown Flood
ACTIVITIES

LESSON NO. 2

In Class

1. Would you rather be in a fire or a flood? Give three reasons for your answer.

    I would rather be in a _____ because:

    a. _____

    b. _____

    c. _____

2. Class discussion on: (1) Pro's and con's of building homes and businesses on lake and river waterfronts; (2) Benefits and drawbacks of flood insurance.

At Home

1. Write a six-word headline about the Johnstown flood.

2. Write a short (100 words) newspaper article about what happened in Johnstown on May 31, 1989.

At the Library

1. In July, 1993, one of the worst floods in history took place in half a dozen states along the Mississippi River and its tributaries. Check with the librarian for articles in newspapers and news magazines describing the flood. Then discuss what made this flood different from other floods.

2. Look up the topic of floods and see how many other major floods you can list.

The Great Galveston Gale

Courtesy: San Francisco Library

The date was: September 8, 1900

The place was: Galveston, Texas

Background

These days we take our weather men and women and all of their scientific equipment for granted. How often do we read the weather report in the daily newspaper? How much attention do we pay to the weather forecasts on television or radio? The answer is probably "seldom" unless we are planning some sort of special outdoor event. Yet we all take comfort in the knowledge that if a dangerous storm is headed our way, we will get accurate advance warning from local and federal meteorologists (weather men).

Such was not the case in Galveston in 1900. At that time Galveston was a booming port city on the Gulf of Mexico. Its population was close to 40,000. Miles of wharves handled more than a thousand ships each year. These ships carried most of the nation's cotton crop and millions of tons of grain.

Yet Galveston was not a safe location for a major city. It had been built on a long, narrow island only three miles across with an average elevation of barely four and a half feet. In other words, it was almost sea level.

The people of Galveston were used to the storms that flooded the beaches and streets and sometimes a few houses. So far no major disaster had slowed down the city's steady growth. No one seemed aware that they were living in a city that lay at the mercy of the elements.

The Disaster

Early risers in Galveston Saturday morning, September 8th, 1990, enjoyed a magnificent sunrise with their coffee. Just after dawn, however, a steady rain started. Soon a fierce wind was blowing. The barometer began to fall — and fall — and fall some more. It alarmed local weather bureau chief Isaac Cline. He raced along the beach front in a horse and buggy. Over and over again he shouted a warning to beach residents to leave their homes. Only a few paid any attention to his wise words.

As usual during a heavy storm, waves began to surge into houses at the beach, causing damage and shoving debris into the city. But this time the powerful waves gushed into the streets. They lifted and pulverized house after house. Winds rose to more than a hundred miles an hour. Deadly debris hurtled through the air. Telephone poles toppled. People tried desperately to wade through chest-deep water to safety.

As the hours passed, the wind and waves continued to batter the city. Chimneys fell down. Brick walls collapsed. A 4,000 ton freighter was carried 22 miles from deep water to a mud flat. In the rail yard, hundreds of boxcars full of grain and cotton were tossed about like match boxes.

The poor people! Even those who wanted to flee to the mainland could not. Both bridges were under water. Many who had somehow survived the first intense wave of wind and water clung to pieces of wreckage. Sick, hurt, half-drowned, only a few were somehow able to survive the long dark hours of the night. The rest were blown into the water and washed out to sea or were buried under tons of falling brick and boards. Ninety children died when the wooden walls of the orphanage where they were sheltered fell apart. Not until 10:00 o'clock that night did the wind begin to die down just a bit.

Aftermath

When the storm passed, Galveston was a ghost town. An eerie silence settled over the wreckage of what was left of the busy seaside city. No one knows for sure how many lives were lost or how many people were washed out to sea or how many were seriously hurt. Estimates are that 6,000 men, women, and children died that night! And more than 5,000 were injured. What is known is that this was by far the greatest toll in any hurricane in the United States.

When the survivors looked around them the next morning, Galveston was in splinters. Half of its buildings had been destroyed, including 2,600 houses. An estimated 10,000 people were homeless. A few homes farther inland came through the storm with only minor damage by a strange twist of fate. Debris from other structures piled up around them and formed a kind of barrier that protected them from the wind.

"We are cast down but not destroyed. Galveston must and shall be rebuilt." So wrote one of the survivors of the 1900 hurricane. This seemed to be a feeling shared by all. The people of the town were determined to rebuild their homes and their city. Within six days a new bridge to the mainland was completed. Badly needed supplies could now arrive by train. Many businesses were open after just a week. Just six weeks later more than three dozen ships were anchored in the harbor. It was once again a busy place as their crews unloaded materials and loaded cotton for exports.

Everyone who could handle a hammer was put to work repairing damaged buildings and constructing new ones. Engineers came up with an interesting plan — they raised 2,000 buildings, mostly houses, about seven feet and set them on beams. Then they filled in the space underneath. In an effort to raise the entire city, about 14 million cubic yards of sand were pumped ashore as a protection against storm tides.

Another measure to shield the city from the Gulf was begun in 1902. It included a great sea wall 3.3 miles long. The wall is constructed of concrete and steel. It stands 17 feet high and is 16 feet wide at its base. Huge boulders lie between it and the sea to weaken wave action.

Today Galveston is one of the greatest cotton and sulfur ports in the world. It also handles products from the West Indies, including raw sugar, bananas, and jute. Its main industries are oil refineries, shipbuilding, dock repair, machine shops, chemicals, fisheries, and the resort and amusement business. Two causeways (roads built over water) now connect the city to the mainland. One is for railroads and the other for motor vehicles.

A number of hurricanes have struck Galveston since 1905 when the wall was finished. But the wall has held and the city stands.

On a separate sheet of paper list all of the underlined words in the story about the Galveston Gale. Find them in the vocabulary section beginning on page 67. Review their meaning and pronunciation. Choose any five and write a sentence for each one.

The Great Galveston Gale
WORD MEANINGS

LESSON NO. 1

The 12 words listed below were all taken from *The Great Galveston Gale* script. Each one has at least two distinctly *different* meanings. Using the dictionary if necessary, write down the dual meanings of each word.

1. case
2. crop
3. down
4. flat
5. bridge
6. wave
7. toll
8. beam
9. head
10. safe
11. chest

The Great Galveston Gale
ACTIVITIES

LESSON NO. 2

In Class

1. Find and discuss the differences or similarities between:

    a. A hurricane

    b. A cyclone

    c. A tornado

    d. A typhoon

2. Make a list of all the words that name a strong or light movement of air. (You should be able to think of at least four or five.)

    _____   _____

    _____   _____

    _____

At Home

You and your family have just heard on the television set that a major hurricane has changed its course and is now headed directly towards you. You have about two hours' warning. You don't want to leave your home, and you decide to stay there to ride out the storm. What are some of the precautions you must quickly take? List at least five.

At the Library

1. A Chinook is a special kind of wind. Where did it get its name? Where is it found? What makes it different from other kinds of winds?

2. Learn all you can about the terrifying hurricane that struck Florida in August, 1992. What was its name? Compare it to the great Galveston gale.

3. Who names hurricanes?

Panic at the Iroquois Theater

The date was: December 30, 1903

The place was: Chicago, Illinois

Background

"The most beautiful theater in the Midwest!" So read the ads for the new Iroquois Theater. "Completely fireproof!" said the building commissioner of Chicago. "Not so!" said a writer in *Fireproof* magazine. His name was William Clendenin. He had toured the theater when it was almost finished. He did not like what he saw. He said there were many flaws in its construction. He called it "one of the worst firetraps in the city." No one in Chicago paid any attention to him.

Courtesy: San Francisco Library

December 30, 1903, was a chilly, dark winter day. Two thousand people filled the Iroquois that afternoon. Most of them were women and children. They had come to see a famous comic, Eddie Foy, in a musical show. The show was a sell-out so the theater was packed. Those who could not get seats stood in the back and in the <u>aisles</u>. The audience loved the first act. They cheered and clapped. Now everyone settled back to enjoy the second act.

The Disaster

A stagehand spotted the first small flicker of fire. He was standing backstage. He watched a piece of <u>flimsy</u> scenery blow against a hot spotlight. Then to his horror, he saw it catch fire. He quickly tried to snuff out the tiny flame but it was just out of his reach. A theater fireman grabbed a fire extinguisher but it, too, could not reach the fast-spreading flame. Within just a few seconds most of the scenery on the stage was on fire. Eddie Foy rushed to the front of the stage. He begged the audience to stay calm, and he almost succeeded. But then someone screamed "Fire!" And the <u>fatal</u> panic began.

Even then the fire might have been held just to the stage. All that was needed was for someone to lower the fireproof <u>asbestos</u> curtain. A stagehand pushed the right buttons to do this. The curtain began to lower but stuck half-way down. In a flash the unchecked fire leaped from the stage into the front rows of the theater. Then all of the lights went out, and panic in the audience exploded.

From then on the situation quickly grew worse and worse. Backstage, members of the cast found they could escape through a back door. When they opened it, this caused a strong draft that fanned the fire. In seconds it roared through the first floor of the theater. Then it split in two. Some of the flames leaped to the balcony. Many people jumped or fell or were pushed from the balcony. Some were on fire as they fell, setting fire to those on whom they landed.

A few people who had been watching the show from the balcony did manage to find an emergency door. It opened onto a fire escape. But there were no ladders from the fire escape to the ground. So people simply jumped, breaking arms and legs. Some were killed when other jumpers fell on top of them. Painters were working in the building across the alley. They placed boards from their building to the fire escape. They saved 12 people in this way until the boards caught fire. Other people in the balcony did manage to find the stairs. It did them little good. The stairs were already jammed with a screaming mob. People could not move down the stairs because of the panicked mass below.

Meanwhile the path of the fire had roared on under the balcony, into the lobby, and up the stairs. Everything blazed — wood seats and trim, drapes, decorations, and the clothes people were wearing.

By this time the audience had turned savage. People fought and clawed as they tried to find exits. Those who stumbled and fell were trampled to death. The young ushers were no help at all. They had not been told what to do in an emergency. They cannot be blamed for their panic and for trying to save their own lives. But this meant there was no one to point the way to emergency doors. Many doors were locked or opened inward. There were no exit signs. People screamed and pushed and shoved and died. The fire raged on and on.

Aftermath

It is hard to believe that the inferno lasted only 15 tragic minutes. When it was over, the walls of the building still stood. The inside looked as if it had been struck by a bomb. When firemen entered the burned-out shell, they found bodies six deep piled in the aisles and doorways. The clothing of many of these poor frantic people had been completely torn off in the mob's desperate fight to escape the smoke and flames. In a very few cases some people were found alive. They had been buried under the bodies of others who had died from the flames or the wild panic of the crowd. The death toll kept going up and up. It finally reached 591 men, women, and children. Hundreds more were badly burned or crushed.

Twelve people were indicted by a Grand Jury on charges of manslaughter. Among these were the owners of the theater, Will Davis and Harry Powers. Also indicted was Building Commissioner Williams. The commissioner did his best to escape blame. He said that his department did not have enough men or money to do its job of inspecting buildings to be sure they were safe.

Not a single person indicted by the Grand Jury ever went to prison. Clever lawyers managed to see that everyone who had anything to do with the theater or the fire went free. One man who ran a saloon near the Iroquois did spend a few months in jail. His building had been pressed into use as a temporary morgue. He was convicted of robbing the dead of their money and jewels. None of the relatives of those who died or were hurt ever got any money for damages. (How different that would be today!)

Theater owner Powers stayed in the entertainment business until the end of his life. Owner Davis never got over the shock of the tragic fire. He tried to fix up the Iroquois and open it again. But the people of Chicago would have nothing to do with it. It was finally sold and torn down. What about Commissioner Williams who had said the building was safe? He just disappeared as dishonest officials have sometimes been known to do.

On a separate sheet of paper list all of the underlined words in the story about the Iroquois Theater. Find them in the vocabulary section beginning on page 67. Review their meaning and pronunciation. Choose any five and write a sentence for each one.

Panic at the Iroquois Theater
CONFIGURATIONS

LESSON NO. 1

Draw a line from the word to the pattern (configuration) that matches it. Then print the word in the space.

enjoy

fire

scenery

audience

scream

escape

settle

balcony

stairs

Panic at the Iroquois Theater
ACTIVITIES

LESSON NO. 2

In Class

1. Write a letter to your local Fire Department. Ask if someone can come to your school and talk about preventing fires at home and at school.

2. Find out the dates of Fire Prevention Week. Make a poster calling attention to this important week.

At Home

1. Find out if your house or apartment has a fire extinguisher and where it is kept. Then ask an adult to show you how it works.

2. Design an escape route for every member of your family in case of fire. Bring it to class to share.

At the Library

1. The great Chicago fire occurred in 1871. The tragic Triangle Factory fire occurred in New York in 1911. Look up these two terrible events and write a paragraph about each of them. Be sure to include a statement about whether or not you think these fires could happen today. Support your statement with facts.

2. Firefighting in the United States has an interesting history. Look it up and write at least two paragraphs. Contrast firefighting equipment today with firefighting a hundred years ago.

Double Disaster in San Francisco

The date was: April 18, 1906

The place was: San Francisco, California

Background

In 1906 about 400,000 people lived in the lively city of San Francisco. The very rich enjoyed life in large homes. The very poor were crowded into dirty slums. Thieves and criminals of all kinds met and plotted in dark dens on the Barbary Coast. At that time San Francisco was a young, restless city. But it showed signs of great promise and growth.

The evening of April 17th had been much like any other. The famous tenor, Enrico Caruso, had sung at the Grand Opera House. People dined in bright cafés. Some drove along the streets in splendid carriages. Others strolled through town in the mild weather. No one had any idea of the terror that lay ahead.

Courtesy: San Francisco Library

The Disaster

The <u>major</u> shock of the earthquake struck with a rumble and a roar at 5:12 A.M. on Wednesday, April 18th. It was followed by small shocks during the next hour or so. But it was the <u>massive</u> first shock that caused the worst damage. Buildings crumbled and fell all over the city. Huge cracks opened up in streets and sidewalks. Towns north, south, and east of the city also suffered terrible damage. In Santa Rosa 60 miles to the north every brick building collapsed.

Frightened people were awakened by the powerful rumbling and shaking. They rushed from their homes and ran through the streets. Many were killed by falling bricks and beams. Many were buried in fallen buildings. But even greater trouble lay in store.

The great fire that followed the quake did not start in one place. And there was no way it could have been prevented. Lighted oil lamps, stoves, and fireplaces had been tossed about by the quake. Gas mains had split. Electric wires lying in the streets shot off showers of sparks. Boilers exploded. Many small fires started which quickly grew into large ones. Worst of all, the city's water mains had burst. The firemen had no water to fight the fires. And so the flames grew larger and quickly spread. To make matters even worse, a slight wind sprang up. In just a few hours nine major blazes were raging in the city.

As whole neighborhoods burned, terrified people fled from the path of the fire. Some were lucky enough to find ferries and tugboats to take them across the Bay to Oakland (there were no bridges at this time). Others camped on the beaches. Still others raced to the parks and to high ground in the open country. A few dishonest men saw a chance to make money on the disaster. They charged huge sums for a short ferry or hack ride. People who had money were willing to pay any price just to get away from the burning city.

Rich and poor alike were victims. Wealthy sections like Nob Hill burned to the ground. So did poor sections like Chinatown and the Barbary Coast. The fire burned for three days and three nights.

Aftermath

It took many weeks to judge just how much damage had been done, first by the quake and then by the fire. Even then it was only a guess. The full damage could never be known. The death toll was listed at 450 but certainly the count was higher. The bodies of many missing people were simply never found. A few hospitals that were still standing were packed with the injured for weeks and months. Nearly 30,000 buildings had burned or crumbled.

Aid poured in from all over the United States. Individuals sent money and blankets and crates of food. City governments sent railroad cars packed with medical supplies and other items that were in short supply in the ruined city.

The people of San Francisco began to work to rebuild the city at once. Their task must have seemed almost impossible to them but they went ahead anyway. First to get attention was the water system. Water trucks had been sent from other parts of the state. This helped a bit although the fear of fire was always present. When it was finished, the new water system was much better than the old. Now there was one system for the public to use, and a separate one for fighting fires.

Ships and trains brought lumber and other building materials. Adults and children worked side by side to clean up the rubbish. Perhaps the amount of the work to be done was good therapy. Perhaps as the citizens of San Francisco worked and struggled and labored, it took their minds off the terrible thing that had happened to them all. In three years they were able to stand back and look with pride at their city restored to its former promise of glory. Since then it has become one of the most beautiful cities in the world visited by thousands of tourists every year.

It should be understood that at the time of the earthquake in 1906, the famous Richter Scale now so widely used to measure the strength of earthquakes was not yet in existence. And so no one knows for certain how strong the quake was. Geologists believe that it was probably close to an 8.0.

As recently as 1989 San Francisco suffered a 6.9 quake which caused major damage and loss of life. A serious fire broke out in the Marina district and quickly spread to a number of buildings. Once again the fire department had water problems caused by broken mains. But this time firemen were able to run a hose from a fireboat off shore and use Bay water to put out the flames. One of the most unbelievable sights after this quake was the Bay Bridge. A huge chunk from the top level tumbled onto the lower level. People had to use ferries for weeks to travel from Oakland to San Francisco until the bridge was repaired. Another tragedy came when a double-decked freeway collapsed. Dozens of people were crushed when the upper deck of the freeway pancaked onto the lower deck. Towns south of San Francisco that were near the epicenter of the quake suffered much greater damage than the city did. Once again it was a terrifying experience. It has caused many people to "quakeproof" their homes and lay in food and water and medical supplies so that they will be ready if another quake comes. And scientists are sure that another quake lies ahead although no one can predict exactly when.

On a separate sheet of paper list all the underlined words in the story about the disaster in San Francisco. Find them in the vocabulary section beginning on page 67. Review their meaning and pronunciation. Choose any five and write a sentence for each one.

Double Disaster in San Francisco
BREAK THE CODE

LESSON NO. 1

The following questions are in code. Break the code by changing each letter to the one that precedes it in the alphabet. Then write your one-word answer in the same code.

1. XIJDI DBNF GJSTU — UIF GJSF PS UIF FBSUIRVBLF?

2. XIBU UPPL QFPQMF BDSPTT UIF CBZ?

3. IPX MPOH EJE UIF GJSF CVSO?

4. XIFSF EJE DSJNJOBMT IBOH PVU?

5. XIBU IBQQFOFE JO TBOUB SPTB?

6. XIZ XBT UIFSF OP XBUFS?

7. IPX TPPO XBT UIF DJUZ SFCVJMU?

8. XIBU EPFT UIF SJDIUFS TDBMF NFBTVSF?

28

Double Disaster in San Francisco
ACTIVITIES

LESSON NO. 2

In Class

Discuss what your class would do if an earthquake struck your town during school hours. Telephones are out. Buses are not running. Include:

1. How you would get home if you lived 5 or more miles from school.
2. How you would treat minor injuries such as cuts and bumps.
3. What it would be like to have to stay at school overnight.
4. What would be the most important item you might have with you.

_____
_____
_____

At Home

People who live in regions where earthquakes are likely to happen are instructed to have certain necessary supplies on hand in case of a major quake. They are told that they might need to be on their own for at least 3 days without help. List 5 things you would need if your home were ever damaged or destroyed by a quake.

_____
_____
_____
_____
_____

At the Library

1. Look up earthquakes in the encyclopedia and write a paragraph about what causes them.
2. Find out all you can about the Richter Scale and the man who invented it.
4. Find some articles about the terrible earthquake in India in September of 1993.

Sinking of the Titanic

The date was: April 15, 1909

The place was: The Atlantic Ocean
(Latitude 41 6′ North
Longitude 50 14′ West)

Background

The world waited eagerly for the launching of the Titanic. Stories about its tremendous size and luxury had appeared in newspapers and magazines in most countries. People felt good that such a comfortable and, most of all, such a safe ship had been designed.

The Titanic was built by Harland & Wolff at their well-known shipbuilding works at Queens Island, Belfast, Ireland. She was 883 feet long and 92½ feet wide. Her eight decks rose to the

Courtesy: New York Times

height of an eleven-story building. All of her machinery and equipment were the finest that could be found at that time.

She was fitted with sixteen lifeboats, each 30 feet long, enough for about 1,200 people (or 75 to a boat). Why were there not more? Because the owners had decided to sacrifice lifeboats in favor of more deck space for the passengers. And why not? The Titanic had been called "unsinkable." This surely was true in light of the safety precautions that were included in her design.

The Titanic's crew numbered 860. There were engineers, wireless operators, boilermakers, navigators, stewards and stewardesses, firemen, ordinary seamen, and officers. There was also a window cleaner, a linen keeper, a stenographer, a fish cook, a soup cook (with assistant), a roast cook, a vegetable cook, an iceman, plate washers, bakers, and a night watchman. All were dedicated to providing every comfort to the 2,208 passengers on the maiden voyage to New York. The trip was to take five days. The time would be enjoyed in luxurious staterooms (some even with fireplaces!). Fine food and wines and entertainment of all sorts were provided. The ship had its own library and a swimming pool (most uncommon on ships in the early 1900's).

The Titanic sailed from Southampton, England, on April 10, 1909, shortly after noon. Her captain was E.J. Smith, a man of vast experience in the Royal Navy Reserve and the White Star Steamship Line. How much of the disaster was Captain Smith's fault? There are many different opinions about this. None can be proven since Captain Smith went down with the Titanic.

The Disaster

The weather during the first few days of the voyage was calm and beautiful. There was no hint of the disaster that lay ahead.

Fred Fleet, a lookout on duty, was the first to spot the iceberg. He later said that had he seen it just a few split seconds earlier, there would have been time to turn the ship away from the huge block of ice. Fleet rang a bell three times. Then he reported to the bridge on the ship's phone, "Iceberg right ahead!" Orders were quickly given to swing the boat to port (left). Then there was a jolt. It was so slight that at first everyone thought they had missed the iceberg altogether. They were wrong! The iceberg had torn a 300-foot gash in the hull of the ship on the starboard (right) side. In minutes six watertight compartments were filled with sea water. The ship was doomed!

A word about how icebergs can cause such tragic damage. When snow falls on a glacier, the pressure forces ice out from the snow particles and presses in air instead. This produces a tight, dense structure that over time gets harder and harder — almost like a rock. Most icebergs are about 3,000 years old. The older they are, the harder they get.

Once it became clear that the Titanic could not survive, the wireless operators were told to send out the new distress call — SOS. By this time the ship was beginning to list (tip) forward (towards the front). The ship Carpathia answered the call. But it was so far away, it could not reach the Titanic until dawn.

The decks were filled with confused, frightened passengers. People ran this way and that. There was panic. There was heroism. Somehow crew members managed to get most of the lifeboats launched in an upright position. One crew member was assigned to each lifeboat. It was then filled with women and children. Many of them were forced to stand because each boat was so crowded.

The nightmare was far from over. People in the lifeboats watched in horror as the Titanic tipped almost on end and began to slip under the water. They could hear the hiss of the boilers, the sounds of the orchestra still bravely playing, and the cries of the drowning. Finally at 2:20 A.M. waves closed over the giant ship. Victims floated all around the lifeboats — some in lifejackets, some clutching onto deck chairs and other pieces of debris. The lifeboat survivors pulled as many as they could out of the freezing water. Often they could not reach the suffering folk in time. They had to watch helplessly as frozen bodies dropped out of sight beneath the black water.

The Titanic had carried more than 2,200 passengers and crew. Only 711 of these, wet and chilled, bobbed around the ocean in the packed lifeboats during the endless night.

At dawn, sea and wind were rising. The lifeboats were in danger of capsizing. The rescue ship Carpathia got there just in time. Bosun's chairs were lowered for those unable to climb the rope ladders. Once on board, people began to search for loved ones. It was hard to give up hope. "Could not another ship have picked them up?" "Is it not possible that they might have climbed on an iceberg?"

Many of the lifeboat survivors were hustled down to the Carpathia's hospital. Others were wrapped in blankets and given hot drinks. Still others crowded into the wireless rooms to send messages to loved ones in the United States and England.

The Carpathia cruised round and round the area, hoping to pick up people clinging to wreckage. None were found. It had been bound for Gibraltar. This was now out of the question. It changed course and headed for New York. Surrounded by tugs, the Carpathia finally unloaded its pathetic passengers at the Cunard pier in New York. It was just eight days after they had left Southampton in such high spirits. Oddly enough, most of the survivors, despite their ordeal in the intense cold, were in good health except for frost-bite and shattered nerves.

Aftermath

Courts of Inquiry into the sinking of the Titanic were held in both the United States and England in an effort to fix blame for the tragedy. Blame was spread equally on a number of factors: the lack of adequate lifeboats, incorrect use of the wireless, bad design of the ship, poor response of ships in the area, speed of the Titanic, overconfidence of its captain, etc.

In September, 1985, after years of intensive search, the wreck of the Titanic was discovered. It was photographed by a special device called an Argo. This new instrument carried cameras and powerful lights to the bottom of the sea. It took pictures of the Titanic's hull, crow's nest, funnels, and many objects — dishes, trays, bottles, bedsprings. After long debate the decision was made, at least for the time being, to leave the wreck undisturbed in its tragic watery grave.

On a separate sheet of paper list all of the underlined words in the story about the Titanic. Find them in the vocabulary section beginning on page 67. Review their meaning and pronunciation. Choose any five and write a sentence for each one.

Sinking of the Titanic
IDIOMS

LESSON NO. 1

All of the words in the left-hand columns come from the script of *Sinking of the Titanic*.

1. Draw a line to the word that means the same or almost the same. The first one has been done for you.

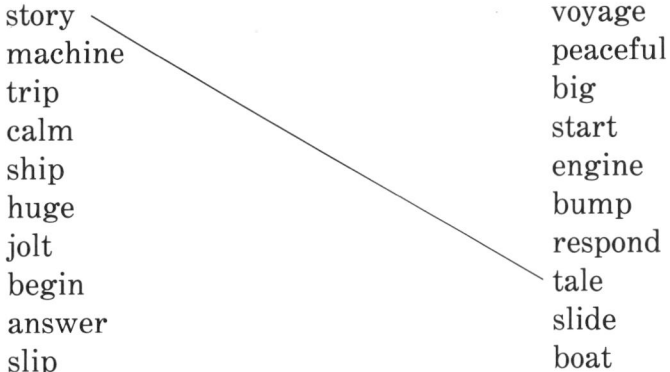

story	voyage
machine	peaceful
trip	big
calm	start
ship	engine
huge	bump
jolt	respond
begin	tale
answer	slide
slip	boat

2. Draw a line to the word that means the opposite. The first one has been done for you.

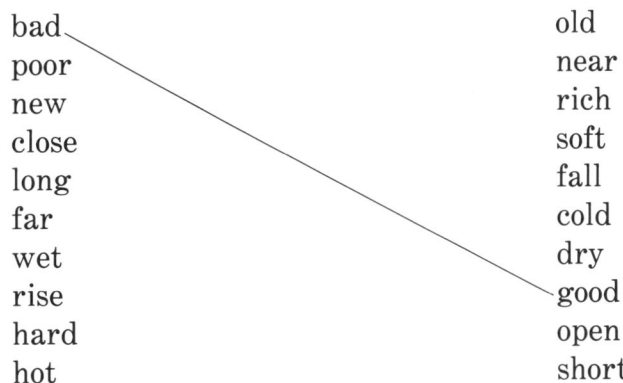

bad	old
poor	near
new	rich
close	soft
long	fall
far	cold
wet	dry
rise	good
hard	open
hot	short

3. Draw a line to the word that has the same sound but a different meaning (homonym). The first one has been done for you.

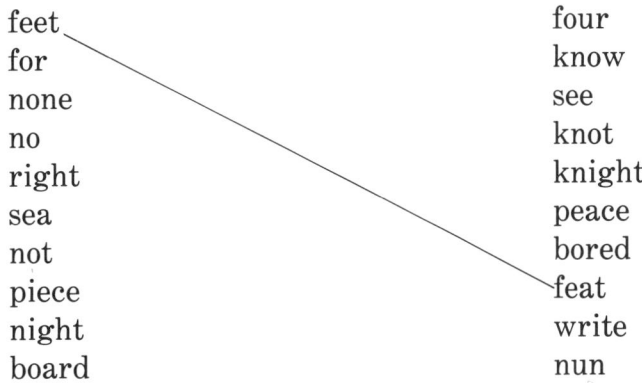

feet	four
for	know
none	see
no	knot
right	knight
sea	peace
not	bored
piece	feat
night	write
board	nun

33

Sinking of the Titanic
ACTIVITIES

LESSON NO. 2

In Class

1. Hold a mock lifeboat drill. Take turns being the officer who gives safety instructions to the passengers (don't panic; women and children first, etc.).

2. Name 8 ships/boats that are used for business or pleasure.
   Name 6 water craft that are used for military purposes.

   _____ _____ _____ _____

   _____ _____ _____ _____

   _____ _____ _____

   _____ _____ _____

At Home

1. Write a telegram (25 words or less) to a family member or friend to say that you were on the Titanic but are safe.

2. Write a paragraph about the coldest you have ever been.

At the Library

1. There have been a number of wartime or peacetime disasters involving large ships. Find out about two or three of these. What caused the disaster? How many lives were lost?

2. Find a copy of the Morse Code. Learn to send an SOS signal.

3. Why do we call ships "she"?

Final Flight of the Hindenburg

The date was: May 6, 1937

The place was: Lakehurst, New Jersey

Background

In the early 1900's people were sure that <u>dirigibles</u> would be the only way to travel by air in the future. These strange new craft had been designed by a German army officer. His name was Count Graf von Zeppelin. That is why dirigibles were often known as "zeppelins." The balloon part of the ship was called the envelope. It looked

Courtesy: Associated Press

like a huge silver cigar. Passengers traveled in cabins that hung below the envelope. These cabins were called gondolas.

By the 1930's many people wished to travel across the Atlantic. And they wanted to do it often. Some traveled for business. Others traveled just for pleasure. At that time they had little choice of transportation. Ocean liners took too long. Lindbergh had made his flight 10 years earlier. But airplanes could still carry only one or two passengers. In those days no one dreamed that planes would ever carry more than just a few people at one time. A dirigible, on the other hand, could carry more than 100 people. And it could carry them in great style and comfort.

In 1937 the Hindenburg was the largest dirigible ever built. It was also said to be the safest. It was 146 feet high and 803 feet long. Its huge envelope was filled with hydrogen. This is one of the most <u>inflammable</u> gases.

Great thought had been given to be sure the passengers enjoyed their trip. <u>Elegant</u> staterooms promised a good night's rest. There was also a music room, a library, a dining room, and an observation deck. Most important of all was a smoking room. Passengers could smoke only in this room. They had to pass through two heavy doors to get to it. They were checked when they left the room to be sure they were not carrying a lighted cigarette. All of this caution was necessary because the envelope held 7,300 cubic feet of hydrogen. Just one spark could cause the whole ship to go up in flames. Many other rules were made to keep the Hindenburg safe. Crew members watched to be sure that these rules were always kept.

Eighteen Atlantic crossings were planned for the Hindenburg in 1937. On May 2nd it left Germany for the first of these trips. In command was Captain Max Pruss. The voyage across the ocean was calm. The passengers were served fine meals. They enjoyed restful sleep. The view from the observation deck was superb.

The Hindenburg was slightly late because of head winds. Otherwise the trip was trouble free. All the passengers agreed that it had been a perfect crossing. They could hardly wait to tell their friends about it.

The Hindenburg was due to end its journey at a tall <u>mooring</u> mast at Lakeland Air Station in New Jersey. But then Captain Pruss heard that thunderstorms were nearby. He cruised outside the area of the storm for three hours. Finally the weather cleared. <u>Visibility</u> was excellent. The Hindenburg moved close to the mooring mast at Lakehurst. It dropped its landing ropes. Passengers waved from the windows. Their friends and families waited on the ground below to greet them.

The Disaster

All at once the peaceful scene was shattered! At first a few people saw a tiny blaze near the tail of the ship. Then, in split seconds, flames swept over the entire silver envelope. Almost at once the ship's fiery tail began to drop to the ground. People standing under the Hindenburg ran for their lives. Passengers in the gondola were knocked to the floor. When they saw the flames, men and women broke windows and began to jump. Some were killed from the plunge to the ground. Others died when flaming <u>debris</u> fell on them. A few seconds later the great dirigible finally crashed to the ground. Passengers and crew tried their best to escape. They had to make their way through roaring flames and thick black smoke. Some made it to safety. Others did not. Captain Pruss beat out his burning clothes with his hands and returned to the ruins again and again to bring people out of the <u>inferno</u>.

A few people escaped only by what can be called a miracle. Joseph Spah, an acrobat, knocked out a window in the gondola. The ship was still 100 feet from the ground. This was too great a height to jump. Spah climbed out of the window. He hung onto a ledge with one arm until the gondola dropped closer to the ground. Then he was able to jump safely. Several other men saw what he was doing. They tried the same plan of escape. But without the strong arms of an acrobat, they could not hold onto the ledge and fell to their deaths.

Werner Franz was a 14-year-old cabin boy. As he jumped to the ground, he glanced up. He saw to his horror that parts of the flaming envelope were about to fall on him. He had no strength to move and braced himself for the end. Just then one of the dirigible's water tanks burst and covered him with cold water. He was then able to scramble to safety with only minor burns.

Eyewitnesses to the tragedy did not always agree on what had happened. Some were sure they had heard explosions. Others thought they had heard noises that sounded like bullets. But there was agreement that the huge envelope had burned completely in just seconds. In fact, it was only 34 seconds after the first tiny flame was spotted that the Hindenburg hit the ground. Sixteen passengers and 20 crew members died in the crash.

Aftermath

What caused the calamity? Experts in the United States and Germany differed on some points and agreed on others. Some thought a spark of static electricity ignited the hydrogen. Some thought it might be sabotage. Lightning was also considered. Still others thought a steel wire might have punctured a cell of hydrogen.

Whatever the cause of the crash of the Hindenburg, the results were final. It was the end of the age of the airship. No dirigible ever again was used to carry passengers across the Atlantic.

———————

On a separate sheet of paper list all of the underlined words in the story about the Hindenburg. Find them in the vocabulary section beginning on page 67. Review their meaning and pronunciation. Choose any five and write a sentence for each one.

Final Flight of the Hindenburg
CATEGORIES

LESSON NO. 1

Many of the words below come from the script of the *Final Flight of the Hindenburg*. Underline the word in each line that doesn't belong.

1.	plane	helicopter	bird	dirigible
2.	trip	voyage	plane	journey
3.	hydrogen	water	oxygen	helium
4.	ocean	lake	bank	river
5.	envelope	flame	fire	blaze
6.	captain	spark	major	general
7.	year	friend	pal	chum
8.	steel	iron	brass	frame
9.	wire	string	cigar	cord
10.	storm	boy	lad	fellow
11.	ground	earth	rope	dirt
12.	men	debris	women	people
13.	strange	odd	unusual	tail
14.	door	window	wall	family
15.	trouble	second	third	first
16.	passenger	lunch	breakfast	dinner
17.	seconds	clothes	minutes	hours
18.	jump	hands	hop	skip
19.	view	cabin	cottage	house

Final Flight of the Hindenburg
ACTIVITIES

LESSON NO. 2

In Class

1. The first letter of eight things that go up in the air is given below. Complete the words.

   P _____ (1 point)   R _____ (3 points)

   B _____ (2 points)   H _____ (2 points)

   D _____ (1 point)   S _____ (2 points)

   K _____ (2 points)   G _____ (3 points)

   Possible Score: 16 points

2. Herbert Morrison, a radio announcer from Chicago, was at Lakehurst the day the Hindenburg crashed and burned. His radio broadcast of that event has become famous. Take turns pretending to be a radio announcer covering the Hindenburg disaster. See who can add the most drama and excitement to their description.

At Home

1. Write a description of a dirigible so that a blind person would know what it looks like.

2. Compare riding in an airplane with riding in a dirigible. What is: noisier, faster, more comfortable, safer, etc.? Which do you prefer? Why?

At the Library

1. Look up Count von Zeppelin. Write a short biographical sketch (2 paragraphs) about his life.

2. Are there any dirigibles in use today? What are they used for?

3. Using newspapers and news magazines, find out exactly where and why a small dirigible crashed in New York in July, 1993.

Fire Storm at the Circus

The date was:
July 6, 1944

The place was:
Hartford, Connecticut

Background

The main tent of Ringling Brothers and Barnum & Bailey Circus had been put up on a huge vacant lot in Hartford. The tent was oval shaped. It was held up by six giant poles. Like all tents, it was made out of canvas. This is an extremely inflammable fabric.

Courtesy: Associated Press

The show started on time in the Big Top at 2:00 o'clock on a sizzling hot July afternoon. Six thousand people, more than half of them children, were enjoying the clowns and the animal acts. The circus had been advertised in posters all over town. It was known as "The Greatest Show on Earth." And it was living up to its promise! Now the happy crowd was waiting for a thrilling high wire act to begin. It was called the Flying Wallendas. The acrobats were already in place way up near the ceiling of the tent.

The Disaster

The fire began as a tiny flame. No one noticed it at first. Then it spread to a side wall of the tent. Suddenly a woman spotted it and exclaimed, "Fire!" Three ushers were standing nearby. They each grabbed a bucket of water and rushed over to the blazing canvas. But they were too late. Already the fire was too big and too hot for them to get near enough to put it out.

At the start, everyone sat quietly. Surely someone would come and put out the fire. Then the circus could go on, and the acrobats could begin. But when the blaze quickly grew to 10 feet, people began to leave their seats. They made their way towards the exits in quiet, orderly fashion. There was no panic. But then the flames, with incredible speed, reached the top of the tent. Huge chunks of burning canvas began to fall. It was then that terror took over the crowd.

The band began to play "Stars and Stripes Forever." This is a signal of danger to circus people. It tells them that help is needed right away. But by this time there was little that anyone could do. A sudden wind had blown in through the main entrance. This fanned the flames, and the fire spread even faster. All of the exits were quickly blocked by the rush of terrified people. Some exits had already been blocked by animal cages. Many people ran to the center ring of the circus hoping to find an exit that way. If they fell — and many did —they were trampled to death. Others were set on fire when huge blazing blankets of canvas fell on them. One by one the thick poles that held up the tent toppled and crushed people under them. Screaming children and their parents could not hold onto one another in the awful mob. The Flying Wallendas at the top of the tent slid down ropes. Then they climbed over a steel cage and ran from the flames. They could do this because they were in top physical condition.

It is hard to believe that the fire lasted only 10 minutes. Someone had called the Hartford Fire Department. It reached the terrible scene quickly. But it was too late — much too late. The firemen could do nothing but turn their hoses on the smoking ruins of the tent. And what they saw and heard shocked them. Frightened animals were making a terrible racket. Crying children dashed here and there looking for their mothers. Hurt and dying people lay everywhere. Men and women sat on the ground not moving. They were clearly in a state of deep shock.

News of the fire came over the radio. People who heard it rushed to the scene to try to find their families who had gone to the circus. It was a time of great joy when missing relatives were found. It was a time of terrible shock and sorrow when their burned bodies were discovered. More than half of the 168 people who died and the 480 who were badly hurt were children. All the rest were women.

It took days to identify all the victims. Finally all the bodies but one were identified. This was a little girl about six years old. No one ever claimed her. The police could never understand why no one reported a missing child. The attempt to identify her went on for months. But the police finally had to give up. She was buried by the City of Hartford. For many years policemen put flowers on her grave on Christmas, Memorial Day, and July 6th, which was the anniversary of the tragic fire.

Aftermath

Fingers of blame were pointed in all directions. The circus owners were accused in a report written by State Attorney Alcorn. The report said that they had not provided enough firefighting equipment in or near the Big Top. Also, they had allowed many exits to be blocked by large cages. Worst of all, the canvas tent had not been properly fireproofed.

At first an electrical short circuit was thought to have started the fire. Some thought that a lighted cigarette that had been carelessly tossed might have done it. But no one really knew the cause of the fire. Finally, six years later, a 20-year-old man, Robert Segel, confessed that he had started the fire. In 1944 at the time of the fire he had been only 14 years old. This was by far the worst but not the only fire he had set. He claimed he had also torched a store, a school, and several other buildings. Why? He said a fiery red rider in his dreams made him do it. This strange young man clearly had deep mental problems. He was given a prison term of 2 to 20 years. Many people thought his sentence was extremely light. Those who lost family members in the fire were very bitter.

They showed their bitterness by <u>suing</u> the owners of the circus. These turned out to be honest men. They paid every single claim. The claims totalled more than $4,000,000. Only $500,000 of this amount was covered by insurance. The rest was paid from the profits from the circus for the next 10 years.

One important change resulted from the Hartford circus fire. Circuses were no longer held in tents. Today circuses are held in stadiums and coliseums and ballparks.

On a separate sheet of paper list all of the underlined words in the story about the Fire Storm at the Circus. Find them in the vocabulary section beginning on page 67. Review their meaning and pronunciation. Choose any five and write a sentence for each one.

Fire Storm at the Circus
WORD SCRAMBLE

LESSON NO. 1

Unscramble the letters to form words from the *Fire Storm at the Circus* script. Write the words in the spaces to the right.

1. T C A A N V — V _ _ _ _ _
2. N L O W C — C _ _ _ _
3. R I E F — F _ _ _
4. T A B R O C A — A _ _ _ _ _ _
5. S V A N A C — C _ _ _ _ _
6. O L E E P P — P _ _ _ _ _
7. G N E A R D — D _ _ _ _ _
8. T X I E — E _ _ _
9. I O A R D — R _ _ _ _
10. S C C U I R — C _ _ _ _ _
11. C L O P I E — P _ _ _ _ _
12. C H O K S — S _ _ _ _
13. S C E U A — C _ _ _ _
14. N E T T — T _ _ _
15. M E A L F — F _ _ _ _
16. Z E L A B — B _ _ _ _
17. A T E S — S _ _ _
18. T A H E R — H _ _ _ _
19. N W T O — T _ _ _
20. S T R O P E — P _ _ _ _ _

43

Fire Storm at the Circus
ACTIVITIES

LESSON NO. 2

In Class

1. Remember the part in the *Fire Storm at the Circus* script where the little girl was never identified? Make up a story that might explain how this could have happened. Write it down and then tell it to the class.

2. Design a poster advertising a circus that will be held in a fireproof tent.

At Home

1. List eight acts you might expect to see at a circus.

2. List eight food and drink items you might expect to buy at a circus.

At the Library

1. Circuses have been entertaining people in this country and Europe for many years. Find out where and when circuses began and how they are different from the circuses of today.

2. There is a clown school in the United States. Where is it held? How does one qualify to be enrolled? How long does it take to become a clown?

The World Blows Up at Texas City

The date was:
  April 16, 1947

The place was:
  Texas City, Texas

Background

Its location on the Gulf of Mexico made Texas City an important port and a center of industry. Chemical plants, smelters, oil refineries, and warehouses crowded the waterfront. A large part of the 18,000 people who lived there held jobs on the docks. They loaded and unloaded ships all day and all night.

Courtesy: United Press

The pay was good. Texas City hummed with activity.

On April 16th three freighters were being loaded. One of them was a French ship, the Grandcamp. It was not yet fully loaded. Workers had partly loaded the ship with 100-pound bags of ammonium nitrate fertilizer. Huge balls of twine and some oil refining equipment were also part of the cargo that had been brought on board. Not far away were two American freighters. The High Flyer also held almost 1,000 tons of ammonium nitrate fertilizer. The Wilson B. Keene was empty. It was expecting a shipment of flour.

It was a quiet morning. Men and women were at their work or at home. Children were in school. It was a day much like any other day. But it soon became a morning that no one would ever forget.

The Disaster

The first sign of danger was spotted on the French freighter Grandcamp. A workman thought he saw and smelled smoke. It seemed to come from the hold where the fertilizer was stored. He lost no time and reported what he had seen to the ship's captain at once. Water would ruin the valuable cargo, so the captain sealed off the area where the smoking fertilizer was stored. His plan was to try to smother the fire with steam. In this way his costly load would not be lost. But almost at once he knew this would not work. The fire was spreading too fast. At this point the captain stopped worrying about his cargo and thought only of his men.

He sounded the fire alarm and ordered everyone to leave the ship. Fireboats moved into position and began pumping tons of water into the ship. The Texas City Fire Department got there as fast as it could. Its men quickly began to fight the blaze. Hundreds of people flocked to the dock to watch the drama. This proved to be a <u>fatal</u> mistake!

Less than an hour after the small wisp of smoke was first spotted, the Grandcamp blew up. It started a chain reaction that destroyed almost all of Texas City.

The Grandcamp and most of the waterfront buildings and docks simply disappeared. Huge red hot chunks of metal and flaming balls of twine from the ship rocketed through the air. Some landed on oil tanks. These burst into flame and crumpled. The blast caused a giant wave to flood the entire dock area. It washed away cars in a nearby parking lot. It drowned many people who were running from the blast.

The High Flyer and the Wilson B. Keene were smashed together like toys. Some of their crew members were killed instantly. Two small planes were knocked out of the sky by flying chunks of metal. The giant Monsanto chemical company exploded. Pipelines burst. Warehouses collapsed. Fire trucks were tossed about like empty soda cans. Homes and schools were not spared. Their walls caved in. Every window in town was shattered. Doors were blown off their hinges. The spinning chunks of metal tore holes in buildings miles from the blast.

Electric wires and water pipes were wiped out. The town had no light or water. This meant there was no way to put out the dozens of fires. In a short time two miles of waterfront buildings were blazing.

Rescuers worked all through the day trying to put out fires and to help the injured. There were many acts of great courage. Then during the evening more bad news was heard. A second ship, the High Flyer, was now on fire. By this time the town <u>officials</u> knew how dangerous ammonium nitrate could be. They ordered everyone to leave the area. Early the next morning the High Flyer exploded. It ripped the Wilson B. Keene in half. Many buildings that had escaped the first blast were now destroyed. A ten-car train was lifted and smashed. Fires and explosions continued through the night.

Aftermath

At last the city grew quiet. It was a ghost town. People wandered around in a daze. Many wept as they looked for members of their family. Now a terrible job lay ahead: to count the dead and the injured. Days later the bad news was read in newspapers all over the country. The total dead was a staggering 561. And 3,500 people had injuries ranging from slight to severe. Hospitals that were still standing could not begin to handle all of the hurt people. Many of the worst cases were moved to hospitals in nearby Galveston and Houston.

Most of those killed were men who were the sole support of their families. This meant that wives and children suddenly found themselves without any income. The husbands and fathers who had left for work that morning would never be coming home.

Chemical plants, <u>refineries</u>, freight yards on the waterfront — all were gone. Men who had lived through the blast suddenly had no jobs. It seemed as if the city itself were dead. And many people were sure it could never be brought back. They were wrong. Texas City began to spring to life again when the head of the Monsanto Chemical Company made an announcement. He said that its Texas City plant would be rebuilt and would be bigger and better than ever. Work would begin at once on it. Other businesses took heart from this announcement and followed Monsanto's lead. People flocked to Texas City to help with the rebuilding. In one year the population grew to 27,000. Hundreds of new houses were built. Hundreds more were repaired. Industry along the waterfront was back in operation. Ships were arriving to be unloaded and loaded as they always had. That meant plenty of jobs.

In three years the city was better than it had ever been. City government and dozens of industries had planned and worked together. New homes, streets, schools, and public buildings gave the city a clean, fresh look. They also lifted everyone's spirits.

One change of greater importance than all of the rest took place. A law was passed forbidding the storage or loading of ammonium nitrate fertilizer. Texas City had learned its lesson well.

On a separate sheet of paper list all of the underlined words in the story about Texas City. Find them in the vocabulary section beginning on page 67. Review their meaning and pronunciation. Choose any five and write a sentence for each one.

The World Blows Up at Texas City
PUTTING FACTS IN ORDER

LESSON NO. 1

Place a "1" next to the sentence that describes what happened first in the script of *The World Blows Up at Texas City*, a "2" next to the sentence that describes what happened next in the script, and so on.

_____ The Grandcamp captain sealed off the area where the smoking fertilizer was stored.

_____ Hundreds of people flocked to the dock to watch the blaze.

_____ Two miles of waterfront buildings caught on fire.

_____ The Grandcamp captain ordered everyone off the ship.

_____ Buildings that escaped the first blast were now destroyed.

_____ The Monsanto Chemical Company made an announcement.

_____ Workers were loading the Grandcamp with 100-pound bags of ammonium nitrate fertilizer.

_____ The Grandcamp blew up!

_____ In three years Texas City was better than it had been before.

_____ Fireboats began pumping tons of water onto the Grandcamp.

_____ Huge hot chunks of metal flew through the air.

_____ A Grandcamp workman thought he saw and smelled smoke.

_____ Early the next morning the High Flyer exploded.

_____ The Grandcamp captain sounded a fire alarm.

_____ The Grandcamp worker reported the fire to the ship's captain.

The World Blows Up at Texas City
ACTIVITIES

LESSON NO. 2

In Class

1. List three more things you would like to know about the Texas City disaster.

   _____
   _____
   _____

2. Include these three questions in a letter to the Texas City Chamber of Commerce. Mention that you are studying the Texas City explosion and you would like to know how the city is doing today.

At Home

1. Write a paragraph explaining how oil spills harm the environment.

2. Ammonium nitrate fertilizer caused the Texas City disaster. Make a list of things in our daily lives that can explode.

At the Library

The economy of Texas City has always depended largely on its oil refineries and chemical plants that use petroleum in their products. Oil keeps Texas City prosperous. Find out all you can about early oil exploration in Texas. Be sure to read about the day the first oil "gusher" came in. It's a fascinating story.

Eruption at Mount St. Helens

The date was: May 18, 1980

The place was:
   Mount St. Helens
      State of Washington
      National Park

Background

Snow-capped Mount St. Helens has long been the crown in a land of beauty. Its slopes were covered with thick forests. Its valleys held rich farms and lush fields of hay. A calm lake and two rivers full of fish were popular vacation spots. Camp sites, picnic grounds, lodges, and homes dotted the landscape.

Courtesy: U.S. Geological Survey

The Indians had many names for the mountain. Such names as Tah-one-lat-clah (Fire Mountain) show that volcanic activity took place long before the pioneers came. In 1792 a British explorer, Captain George Vancouver, named the dormant volcano. He used the last name of the man who was then the British ambassador to Spain.

Scientists were watching the volcano in March, April, and May of 1980. They not only felt but they saw minor quakes with flying and molten rock. Their reports caused the Governor to call a state of emergency. The U.S. Forest Service closed roads. Tourists were kept out of the region. A few days later when the volcano seemed quieter home owners and workers were allowed to return. But no one was permitted within 10 miles of Mount St. Helens.

By mid May things began to look worse. This time Governor Ray gave homeowners only four hours to pack up and leave. It was a hard decision for the Governor to make. Most people did not want to leave. But it was a wise move. Many lives were saved because of it.

The Disaster

It is hard to describe an explosion that had a force 500 times greater than the atom bomb that destroyed the Japanese city of Hiroshima at the end of World War II. The savage Mount St. Helens eruption on May 18th at 8:32 A.M. was touched off by a 5.1 earthquake. Its north side simply vanished down the side of the mountain. Hot gas, ash, and huge rocks shot into the air. This started a scorching avalanche. It quickly grew to a width of 12 miles and slashed through all the forests in its path. Two-hundred mile winds knocked down thousands and thousands of trees. Those that were left were set on fire by falling hot ash.

Tons of bubbling mud gushed down the mountain at 50 miles an hour. Right in its path was the South Fork of the Toutle River. The avalanche caused a huge wave to form in the river. This wave swept downstream and destroyed everything in its path. Next it poured into Spirit Lake and then into the North Fork of the Toutle. A log jam 200 feet high was formed.

Another boiling mudslide rushed down the slopes as far as the Cowlitz and Columbia Rivers. This slide raised river levels and killed fish. It created new sandbars in rivers that later became a hazard to ships.

Ash from the blast caused problems as far away as 500 miles. The worst effect was felt in the eastern part of the state. States which lay to the east also felt the effects of the eruption since the wind was blowing in that direction. Visibility was so poor, roads were closed. Street lights had to be turned on. All plane flights were cancelled. The thick ash clogged car engines. Motorists had to leave their trucks and cars and make their way through the fallout to the nearest shelter. Some people were sure an atom bomb had fallen.

Millions of tons of gases and ash poured from the mountain all day and most of the night. The horrendous landslide that the explosion caused was the largest ever recorded anywhere in the world.

Aftermath

The height of Mount St. Helens was reduced more than 1,000 feet. Pilots who flew over the region spotted a steaming crater one mile wide. First photographs showed devastation that was hard to believe. As far as the eye could see, it looked like pictures of a bleak moonscape. In mile after mile there was not a single sign of life.

Even with the early warnings, 35 people were killed. Twenty five more were missing. No trace of these 25 were ever found. Half of the state's entire alfalfa crop was destroyed. At first farmers couldn't understand why the wheat harvest nearly doubled. They finally decided that insects which usually damaged the wheat had been killed by falling hot ash. A million and a half birds and animals (deer, bear, elk, beaver, pheasant, quail, etc.) were lost in the volcanic flow. The lakes and rivers were so hot that all fish and other water creatures died.

Clean-up was started at once. Loggers went to work to truck thousands of fallen trees to nearby lumber mills. The Army Corps of Engineers worked overtime to clear the clogged rivers. It took months for towns within 500 miles of Mount St. Helens to get rid of the ash. People swept and washed and swept again. Still the fine grey ash sifted to earth. It covered sidewalks, streets, porches, yards, vegetable and flower gardens, cars — anything that was outside. Medical masks were worn over noses and mouths. Eyes grew red from the gritty ash.

During the next year Mount St. Helens had a number of mild eruptions. Since then it has been calm. Scientists continue to monitor it closely. Recent amazing photographs show that abundant plant and animal life has begun to come back. Deer and other animal tracks have been seen. Birds have slowly begun to nest in the broadleaf trees that were not burned. Many kinds of sturdy plants are pushing their way up through the soil and ash. With each passing year, more and more signs of life can be seen. Scientists say that if there are no more eruptions, the land around Mount St. Helens will regain its full beauty in about 200 years.

On a separate sheet of paper list all of the underlined words in the story about the Eruption at St. Helens. Find them in the vocabulary section beginning on page 67. Review their meaning and pronunciation. Choose any five and write a sentence for each one.

Eruption at Mount St. Helens
FILL IN THE BLANKS

LESSON NO. 1

1. Mount St. Helens is located in _____.
   a. Mexico
   b. California
   c. Alaska
   d. Washington

2. Mount St. Helens was named by _____.
   a. The Governor
   b. The President of the U.S.
   c. A British explorer
   d. Helen Keller

3. In May, 1980, the Governor _____.
   a. ran for election
   b. called a state of emergency
   c. took a trip
   d. levied new taxes

4. The eruption began with a quake that measured _____.
   a. 5.6
   b. 6.1
   c. 7.1
   d. 5.1

5. After the explosion the winds were clocked at _____.
   a. 10 miles an hour
   b. 50 miles an hour
   c. 100 miles an hour
   d. 200 miles an hour

6. The log jam in the North Fork was _____.
   a. 200 feet high
   b. 2,000 feet high
   c. 50 feet high
   d. 100 feet high

7. The landslide from the explosion was _____.
   a. quite small
   b. medium sized
   c. the largest ever recorded
   d. not very impressive

8. The height of Mount St. Helens was reduced by _____.
   a. 10,000 feet
   b. 100 feet
   c. 1,000 feet
   d. 10 feet

9. The blast caused problems as far away as _____.
   a. 5,000 miles
   b. 50 miles
   c. 500 miles
   d. 5 miles

10. Recent photographs show that plant and animal life _____.
    a. has begun to come back
    b. is better than before the blast
    c. has vanished forever
    d. started to come back, but stopped

Eruption at Mount St. Helens
ACTIVITIES

LESSON NO. 2

In Class

1. You are the Governor of the State of Washington. You must go on radio and television to order people out of the area near Mount St. Helens. Write the short speech that you would give explaining the situation to the people in the state, telling them where to go and when they may expect to be able to return to their homes.

   _____
   _____
   _____
   _____

2. Make a list of all the adjectives you can think of that might describe the eruption at Mount St. Helens. Select one class member to write the adjectives on the board to see which one is listed most often.

   _____   _____   _____   _____
   _____   _____   _____   _____
   _____   _____   _____   _____

At Home

1. Pretend that you are in the path of an onrushing avalanche. You must leave your home quickly and can only take three things. Which would you take?

2. Pretend you are in a helicopter looking down at the eruption. Describe in 1 or 2 paragraphs what you see.

At the Library

1. Find out if there have been any more eruptions at Mount St. Helens since May, 1980. If so, how many? When?

2. Another famous volcano is Mount Vesuvius. Where is it? Look it up and write 2 paragraphs about it. Include information about the last time it erupted.

Challenger — Tragedy in the Sky

The date was: January 28, 1986

The place was: Kennedy Space Center, Florida

Background

Courtesy: Topham

In 1969 man walked on the moon. What next? Scientists began to think about a trip to the planet Mars. A direct flight from Earth to Mars was out of the question. But a flight from Earth with a stop at a space station and then onto Mars might be possible. A space station? One would have to be built in space. How could tons of building materials and equipment be ferried into space? A very special kind of vehicle would be needed. And so the idea of a space shuttle was born. The concept was new. Scientists worked for years on the design. The final result was an orbiter that would be shot into space like a rocket.

Great power would be needed to launch such an orbiter. It would have three engines. But that would not be enough. It would also have two rocket boosters. These would be released about two minutes into the flight. They would parachute into the sea and be picked up to be used again. The orbiter would also need a huge fuel tank for launch. This would be empty about eight minutes into the flight. It would separate from the orbiter and burn up. After completing its mission, the space shuttle orbiter could return to Earth and land like an airplane.

Work went on steadily. Eventually NASA had four space shuttles in its fleet. They were the Columbia, Discovery, Challenger, and Atlantis. Columbia was the first of these to go into orbit in April, 1981. But the flight of the Challenger scheduled for early 1986 was to be very special indeed. It had been decided that America's first private citizen would be a passenger on this flight. The President of the United States, Ronald Reagan, made the decision that a school teacher would be chosen for this honor.

More than 10,000 teachers from all over the United States applied. This huge number was finally whittled down to ten. These ten finalists were flown to the Johnson Space Center in Houston, Texas. There they were given medical, physical, and other fitness tests. They then returned to Washington, D.C., where a panel of seven NASA officials announced the winner. It was Christa McAuliffe, a social studies teacher from Concord, New Hampshire. She was overjoyed. So were her students, her family, and the residents of Concord.

Training for the flight began in Houston in the fall of 1985. Christa joined the six other

Challenger crew members for a tough program. She hated to leave her husband Steven and her two children, nine-year-old Scott and six-year-old Caroline. But to go into space was a once-in-a-lifetime opportunity. Everyone in her family felt that she should go.

During the busy days of training Christa found time to keep a journal. She also worked on the lessons and experiments she planned to broadcast live from space. Twenty-five million students in schools all over the United States and Canada would watch her on television.

In addition to studying and learning all about the orbiter and to practicing weightlessness, Christa got to choose the foods she would eat in space. She had a choice of 100 foods and 45 drinks. All were packed in special containers so that they wouldn't float around in the weightless Challenger cabin. Each crew member could choose some personal things to take along. Christa packed her husband's class ring from college, her daughter's cross and chain, and her son's stuffed toy frog.

The launch of the Challenger was postponed several times. Finally, on Tuesday, January 28, the weather was good although very, very cold. Christa and the crew boarded the orbiter. Her parents, sisters, brothers, and families of the other Challenger crew members watched from a viewing stand. Her husband and children watched from the top of a nearby building. Television sets in homes and classrooms all over the country were tuned in to the event. Nine, eight, seven, six, five, four, three, two, one — lift-off!

The Disaster

The orbiter lifted off the ground and soared into space. Everyone cheered and shouted at the beautiful sight. Their pride and joy lasted little more than a minute. Suddenly with no warning the sky was filled with dark smoke and orange fire. The space shuttle orbiter had exploded while Christa's family, the cheering crowd, and the world watched. There was only stunned silence as pieces of wreckage fell to earth. It was the worst tragedy in the history of space flight. America wept as it lowered its flags to half-staff.

President Reagan sent his vice-president to the Kennedy Space Center to be with the families of the Challenger crew. That night on television he spoke of the nation's sorrow. He ended his words by saying, "We will never forget them nor the last time we saw them this morning as they prepared for their journey and waved goodbye... Man will continue his conquest of space, to reach out for new goals... That is the way we shall commemorate our seven Challenger heroes."

The Aftermath

The President appointed a commission at once to find the cause of the tragedy. Teams were sent to recover debris from the ocean. Films of the flight were studied over and over again. Now scientists could see a tiny orange flame flickering on the right-hand booster. This tiny flame ignited hydrogen from the leaking fuel tank which then exploded in a great fireball. The explosion flung the orbiter off course. It spun at a tremendous speed and was torn apart by forces in the atmosphere.

After months of study and listening to experts, the President's commission finally decided that there had been a flaw in the design of the booster rockets. One part in particular called the O-ring had failed. It was thought that the very cold weather may have been the reason for its failure.

Many tributes to Christa and the other members of the Challenger crew followed. Services were held at the Johnson Space Center in Houston, at the Kennedy Space Center in Florida, and at Concord, Christa's home town. Many states started scholarships in Christa's memory to help students who want to become teachers. The United States Department of Education announced that one million dollars would be used to provide Christa McAuliffe scholarships for teachers to study math and science with leading experts.

Foreign governments also seemed moved by the tragedy. Japanese officials and businessmen sent $100,000 to Christa's school, Concord High School. An American bank started a trust fund for the children of the seven Challenger astronauts. These are only a few of the many honors given to Christa and her fellow crew members. The greatest honor to Christa perhaps was that through her efforts — and her death — greater respect has been paid to the teaching profession than ever before.

Equally important, the space program endures. After a long period when scientists and engineers worked to correct design problems, shuttle flights began again. The flight to Mars may yet become a reality!

On a separate sheet of paper list all of the underlined words in the story about the Challenger tragedy. Find them in the vocabulary section beginning on page 67. Review their meaning and pronunciation. Choose any five and write a sentence for each one.

Challenger — Tragedy in the Sky
VOCABULARY

LESSON NO. 1

Many small words can be made from large words. Follow the directions to make small words using the letters in the word *Challenger*. You do NOT have to use the letters in the order in which they appear in the word.

C H A L L E N G E R

Find 2 words that end in "all."

_____   _____

Find 2 five-letter words.

_____   _____

Find 2 words that end in "ng."

_____   _____

Find 2 words that begin with "ch."

_____   _____

Now try this word.

W E I G H T L E S S N E S S

Find 2 words that are numbers.

_____   _____

Find 2 words that have a double "e" in the middle.

_____   _____

Find 2 words ending in "ght."

_____   _____

Find 2 words ending in "w."

_____   _____

Challenger — Tragedy in the Sky
ACTIVITIES

LESSON NO. 2

In Class

1. The United States spends billions of dollars each year on its space program. Some people feel this money could be better spent in other ways. What is your opinion? Write a paragraph explaining your views.

   _____
   _____
   _____
   _____

2. Imagine you have been chosen to go on a space mission. You will be orbiting the earth for three days. Name a famous person you would like to take with you. You must explain the reasons for your choice.

   _____
   _____
   _____

At Home

1. List 3 reasons why you would or would not wish to make a trip into space.

2. Christa McAuliffe chose a number of personal items to take into space. What would you choose? (Remember — your choices cannot weigh more than 24 ounces.)

At the Library

Find out the names of the first group of astronauts. What happened to them? Which ones died in a training accident? Who was the first in space? Who landed on the moon? Which one became a United States Senator?

The Chernobyl Catastrophe

The date was: April 25, 1986

The place was: Chernobyl, USSR

Background

The first clue that something was terribly wrong was discovered in Sweden. Workers at a nuclear power station were alarmed. A detector was showing 100 units of radioactivity. The normal reading was four units! They began to check frantically for a leak. None could be found.

Courtesy: Novosti

At about the same time neighboring countries Denmark and Norway reported that they, too, had found a sudden huge increase in radioactivity. What could be causing it? Scientists began to look at the speed and direction of the wind. It took only a short while for them to track the problem to the nuclear power station in Chernobyl in the Union of Soviet Socialist Republics (now northern Ukraine). It clearly was leaking radioactive material into the atmosphere. The scientists feared that an explosion of some sort had taken place. But why hadn't they heard from the officials in the USSR?

Hours passed. Not a single word came from the Soviet Union about a nuclear accident. Governments all over the world grew angry. Wild rumors began to spread. The Soviet leaders did not even tell their own people what had happened. The people went about their usual daily activities. They had no idea that a killing radioactive cloud was sweeping over their country — a cloud that would poison their food and water and, indeed, the very air they breathed. It was not until 18 days later that Mikhail Gorbachev, head of the Soviet government, spoke on television. He described the disaster and its fallout.

The Disaster

The explosion at Chernobyl has been correctly called "the world's worst nuclear accident." It need not have happened. Workers at the plant were carrying out an experiment. In order to do so, they had to break (or at least bend) some rules. They cut the amount of power needed to operate the plant. They slowed down the coolant pumps. They turned off safety and alarm systems.

Around midnight the coolant water began to boil. This triggered an alarming rapid rise in the <u>reactor</u> <u>core</u> temperature. It also caused a swift uncontrollable surge of power from the reactor. At this point an alert worker hit an emergency shutdown switch. It was too late! The situation was totally out of control. All of the fuel and water pipes in the core overheated, melted, and fell into pieces. Steam explosions caused damage to <u>vital</u> core parts. Worst of all, hydrogen from the core exploded when it made contact with air. Roofs and walls of the building collapsed. Killing radioactive material shot into the atmosphere.

The terrible explosion caused dozens of fires. Burning radioactive debris fell from the sky. A fire started inside the reactor. Local firemen acted bravely but they simply didn't know how to fight a radioactive fire. They tried to control the fires with chemicals and water. But the blaze was so hot, the water turned into radioactive steam. And so things quickly grew worse and worse. Many brave people died. Some were firemen. Some were workers who stayed at their posts in order to shut down the other three reactors in the area. Hundreds of people at the plant got high doses of radiation. Some were flown to a special hospital in Moscow. They could not be saved.

What to do about the fire? It continued to burn and shoot radioactive poison into the air. The officials sent up helicopters. They carried loads of sand and clay to drop on the fire to smother it. The area water supply was also in great danger. A group of engineers came up with a plan. They scooped out a huge tunnel under the burning reactor. They filled the tunnel with concrete. In this way radioactivity could not seep into the earth and poison the water supply. Clean-up of radioactive debris and topsoil has taken years. One of the last steps was enclosing the entire reactor in a concrete box 20 stories high.

Aftermath

The full impact of the Chernobyl disaster cannot yet be told. This is because many people who were near the accident and received radioactive fallout are still reporting cancer and other illnesses. But some things have become known over time. For example, the Chernobyl workers lived in the town of Pripyat. The entire town and the surrounding area had to be evacuated. It took 1,200 buses to move the Pripyat citizens. In all, about 135,000 people had to be moved. They will never be able to return to their homes. However, in one sense, the people around Chernobyl were lucky. The accident happened at night when most people were asleep. It did not rain, so much of the radiation was carried away by the winds. But not enough to save the town!

It is thought that about seven tons of radioactive material was shot into the atmosphere by the Chernobyl <u>calamity.</u> Winds steadily carried this poison all over Europe. Some Polish farm workers were the first to suffer. Rain washed the deadly radiation onto their farms. Their skin itched. Their hair fell out. Their hands swelled. They became very ill. Some died.

Thousands of birds dropped from the sky after flying through the radioactive atmosphere. Grass and crops were ruined. People tried to keep themselves and their children and their animals under cover as much as possible. Trucks, trains, and buildings were hosed down all over Europe. All kinds of crops had to be tested before they were sold or eaten. Many had to be thrown away. A quarter of a million children were evacuated from Kiev, a city 62 miles south of Chernobyl, because a radioactive cloud had passed right over that city. The tourist trade suffered. No one wanted to go to Europe and risk being exposed to radiation.

Bits of radiation remain in the <u>troposphere</u>. Traces of fallout have even been found in the United States. Some scientists believe that in the next 30 years as many as 100,000 Europeans will die from cancer caused by the Chernobyl disaster.

Nuclear power stations are still in use throughout the world. (The United States had its own dangerous accident in 1979 at the Three Mile Island nuclear plant in Pennsylvania. It was, however, not nearly so bad as Chernobyl although local residents had to be evacuated.)

Nuclear power was developed because it would save oil and coal. It is thought that both of these resources will one day run out. But is it safe? Many countries have stopped building nuclear power stations. Some are even being torn down. It's a huge problem. Our country — and other countries — must decide if the benefits outweigh the risks.

On a separate sheet of paper list all the underlined words in the story of the catastrophe at Chernobyl. Find them in the vocabulary section beginning on page 67. Review their meaning and pronunciation. Choose any five and write a sentence for each one.

The Chernobyl Catastrophe
ADD-A-LETTER

LESSON NO. 1

Many words can be changed into new words by adding a letter. For example, see how the word *spot* can be changed to *sport* simply by adding the letter **r**.

Put the letter **t** in each of the following words to make a new word. Write the new word in the space next to the old word.

1. hat _____
2. for _____
3. oil _____
4. one _____
5. his _____
6. plan _____
7. ear _____
8. die _____
9. though _____

Put the letter **k** in each of the following words to make a new word. Write the new word in the space next to the old word.

1. not _____
2. pin _____
3. night _____
4. ink _____
5. plan _____
6. ill _____
7. sun _____
8. as _____
9. new _____

Put the letter **w** in each of the following words to make a new word. Write the new word in the space next to the old word.

1. here _____
2. as _____
3. sift _____
4. no _____
5. edge _____
6. to _____
7. arm _____
8. hen _____
9. sing _____

Put the letter **e** in each of the following words to make a new word. Write the new word in the space next to the old word.

1. to _____
2. had _____
3. far _____
4. hug _____
5. motion _____
6. go _____
7. merge _____
8. quality _____
9. did _____

The Chernobyl Catastrophe
ACTIVITIES

LESSON NO. 2

In Class

1. Choose two teams to debate the topic of nuclear energy. One team will speak in its favor; the other team will speak against it. Be sure to include factors such as cost, pollution, safety, etc.

2. As a class make a list of alternate forms of energy. You should be able to think of at least five, more if possible.

3. What form of energy is used to heat your home, cook your food, drive your car?

At Home

1. List all the times you and members of your family have been exposed to radiation (x-rays at the dentist, etc.). Ask family members for input.

2. Write a paragraph about the positive uses of radiation.

At the Library

The accident at the Three Mile Island nuclear plant is mentioned in *The Chernobyl Catastrophe* script. It is the worst nuclear accident to date in this country. Find out all about it. Where is Three Mile Island nuclear plant? When did the accident happen? What caused it? What happened to the people who lived nearby? What happened to the workers at the plant? Is it still operating?

Vocabulary

Vocabulary

aisle
(īl)

a passageway as between rows of seats
We walked down the aisle to our seats.

anniversary
(ăn-ə-vur′-sə-rē)

the yearly return of the date of an important event
They celebrated the anniversary of their marriage.

asbestos
(ăz-bĕs′-təs)

a fireproof mineral used in roofing, theater curtains, etc.
The fire didn't spread because of the asbestos in the roof.

atmosphere
(ăt′-məs-fēr)

the air surrounding the earth
How thin is the atmosphere 25 miles above the earth?

attempt
(ə-tĕmpt′)

to try to do; to make an effort
He will attempt to set a new world record.

avalanche
(ăv′-ə-lănch)

a large mass of snow or earth sliding down a mountain
The skiers just missed being buried by an avalanche.

barometer
(bə-räm′-ət-ər)

an instrument for measuring atmospheric pressure and thus forecasting weather
Check the barometer to see if it is going to storm.

barrier
(băr′-ē-ər)

anything that blocks or hinders
Forts often had high walls as a barrier against enemies.

booster
(bōōst′-er)

a propulsion unit that supplies extra thrust at the take-off of a space vehicle
They carefully checked the booster before take-off.

bosun
(bō′-sən)

a seaman known as a boatswain
The bosun helped them into the lifeboats.

bridge
(brĭj)

a raised platform running from side to side on a ship for the officers and navigators
The ship's captain stood on the bridge to give his orders.

calamity
(kə-lăm′-ə-tē)

a great misfortune; a disaster
Her house burning down was a terrible calamity.

capsize
(kăp′-sīz)

to overturn or upset, especially a boat
They were thrown into the water when the boat capsized.

cargo
(kär′gō)

the load carried by a ship, truck, etc.
The ship carried a cargo of wheat.

commemorate
(kə-mĕm′-ə-rāt)

to honor the memory of, especially by a ceremony
They put up a statue to commemorate his victory.

commission
(kə-mĭsh′-ən)

a group of people appointed to perform special duties
She was asked to serve on the new commission.

compartment
(kəm-pärt′-mənt)

any of the divisions into which a space is divided
The ship's compartments were supposed to be watertight.

concept
(kän′-sĕpt)

an idea or a thought
Explain your concept of honesty to me.

contaminate
(kən-tăm′-ə-nāt)

to make impure; to pollute
Toxic materials will contaminate the land.

coolant
(kōōl′-ənt)

a fluid for cooling engines
I need to add coolant to my car.

core
(kōr)

the part of a nuclear power reactor that contains the fuel
They inspected the core of the space ship.

debris
(də-brē′)

bits and pieces of fragments, rubbish, etc.
After the accident, they swept up the debris.

dedicate
(děd′-ĭ-kāt)

to set apart for a special purpose
I am going to dedicate my book to my children.

devastation
(děv-əs-tā-shən)

wasted; ruined; destroyed
After the earthquake the devastation was widespread.

dirigible
(dĭr-ə-jə-bəl)

an airship or balloon driven by motors
Have you ever ridden in a dirigible?

dormant
(dôr′-mənt)

inactive; in a resting state
The trees are dormant in the winter.

elegant
(ěl′-ə-gənt)

dignified richness and luxury
The state rooms in the White House are elegant.

elements
(ěl′-ə-məntz)

forces of the atmosphere such as wind, rain, etc.
During the tornado the elements were at their worst.

elevation
(ěl-ə-vā′-shən)

height above the surface of the earth or sea level
The mountain had an elevation of 4,500 feet.

emergency
(ē-mʉr′-jən-sē)

a sudden unexpected event that calls for immediate action
After his heart attack, they rushed him to the emergency room of the hospital.

epicenter
(ĕp′-ĭ-sĕnt-ər)

the area of the earth's surface directly above the place of origin of an earthquake
The scientists were able to pinpoint the epicenter of the quake.

evacuate
(ē-văk′-yōō-āt)

to make empty; to leave or withdraw from a dangerous place
When the dam broke, the people in the town had to be evacuated.

exit
(ĕks-ĭt)

a way out
Be sure that there are signs on all of the exits.

fallout
(fôl′-out)

radioactive materials that fall from the sky
There was massive fallout after the nuclear explosion.

fatal
(fāt′-l)

resulting in death
His fall from the bridge was fatal.

fertile
(fɯrt′-l)

able to produce abundant crops; fruitful
The valley is known for its fertile soil.

flimsy
(flĭm′-zē)

easily broken or damaged
The material in her dress was very flimsy.

flourish
(flɯr′-ĭsh)

to grow vigorously; to thrive
The fertilizer helped the plants to flourish.

frantic
(frăn′-tĭk)

wild with anger, pain or worry
I was frantic that I might miss my plane.

function
(fŭnk′-shən)

to work; to be used
An air conditioner's function is to cool the building.

geologist
(jē-äl'-ə-jĭst)

one who deals with the science of the earth's crust, its rocks and fossils, etc.
The geologist carried his rock samples in a sack.

hack
(hăk)

a taxi
A hack dropped us off at the airport.

heroism
(hĕr'-ō-ĭz-əm)

qualities and actions of courage and bravery
Saving the child from drowning was an act of heroism.

hold
(hōld)

the interior of a ship below deck where cargo is carried
Our trunks are stored in the ship's hold.

horrendous
(hō-rĕn'-dəs)

horrible; awful; frightful
It was a horrendous explosion.

ignite
(ĭg-nīt')

to set fire to; to catch on fire; start burning
Here is a match to ignite the fire.

impressive
(ĭm-prĕs'-ĭv)

causing wonder and admiration
His school records were impressive.

incident
(ĭn'-sə-dənt)

an event; something that happened
The incident took place on a street corner.

incredible
(ĭn-krĕd'-ə-bəl)

too unusual to be possible
The story she told is just incredible!

indict
(ĭn-dīt')

to charge with a crime
He was indicted for armed robbery.

industry
(ĭn'-dəs-trē)

any large-scale business activity
The steel industry hired many workers.

inferno
(ĭn-fûr'-nō)

huge blaze
The small fire quickly turned into an inferno.

inflammable
(ĭn-flăm'-ə-bəl)

quality of catching fire easily and quickly
That fabric is extremely inflammable.

jute
(jo͞ot)

a strong fiber for making rope, etc.
The rope factory placed a big order for jute.

maiden voyage
(mād'-n voi'-ĭj)

first trip
The Titanic hit an iceberg on its maiden voyage.

major
(mā'-jər)

greater in size, amount, importance, etc.
She received a major promotion.

manslaughter
(măn'-slôt-ər)

the unlawful killing of a human being by another
He was arrested and tried for manslaughter.

massive
(măs'-ĭv)

big and solid; large
King Kong was a massive ape.

monitor
(män'-ĭ-tər)

to watch or check on a person or thing
I will monitor her performance.

monstrous
(män'-strəs)

huge; horrible; shocking
He told a monstrous lie.

moonscape
(mo͞on'-skāp)

the surface of the moon
He decided to paint a moonscape.

mooring
(mo͞or-ĭng)

a place where a ship is anchored
He rented mooring space for his yacht.

morgue
(môrg)

place where the bodies of unknown dead are temporarily kept
They had to identify the body at a morgue.

NASA

National Aeronautics and Space Administration
He worked at NASA.

neighboring
(nā'-bər-ĭng)

close by
She lived in a neighboring town.

notice
(nōt'-ĭs)

announcement or warning
The notice was posted on the door.

nuclear
(no͞o-klē-ər)

involving atomic energy
Nuclear energy is clean and cheap.

official
(ə-fĭsh'-əl)

holding a position of authority
The official gave the other team a penalty.

orbiter
(ôr'-bĭt-ər)

the airplane part of the space shuttle that goes into orbit and returns to earth
The orbiter landed in California.

ordeal
(ôr-dēl')

any difficult or painful experience
Crossing the plains in the winter was an ordeal.

orderly
(ôr'-dər-lē)

well-behaved; law abiding
They left the building in orderly fashion.

orphanage
(ôr'-fən-ĭj)

an institution that is a home for children without parents
After his parents died, he was sent to an orphanage.

pathetic
(pə-thĕt′-ĭk)

arousing pity or sorrow
That kitten out in the rain is a pathetic sight.

pilgrimage
(pĭl′-grəm-ĭj)

a journey made to a holy place
They are going to make a pilgrimage to Jerusalem.

pitiful
(pĭt′-ĭ-fəl)

arousing or deserving pity and compassion
Those hungry children look pitiful.

precaution
(prē-kô′-shən)

care taken beforehand against danger, failure, etc.
A shot is a good precaution against flu.

pulverize
(pŭl′-vər-īz)

to grind into small bits or powder
The firecracker pulverized the paper bag.

puncture
(pŭnk′-chər)

a hole made by a sharp point
The tire had a puncture in it.

radiation
(rā′-dē-ā-shən)

rays of sunlight or nuclear particles
He got a large dose of radiation in the blast.

radio activity
(rā′-dē-ō ăk-tĭv′-ə-tē)

sending out nuclear radiation
Be careful — that may be radioactive.

reaction
(rē-ăk′-shən)

a chemical change; a response
He had a bad reaction to the medicine.

reactor
(rē-ăk′-tər)

a device in which a controlled nuclear reaction happens
Each nuclear plant has its own reactor.

reality
(rē-ăl′-ə-tē)

a person, thing, or fact that is real
The reality is that everyone must go to school.

refinery
(rĭ-fīn′-ər-ē)

a plant for purifying materials, as oil, sugar, etc.
They went to a sugar refinery on a field trip.

relative
(rĕl′-ə-tĭv)

a person connected by blood or marriage; family member
My favorite relative is my cousin Sam.

Renaissance
(rĕn-ə-säns′)

the great revival of art and learning in Europe in the 14th, 15th, and 16th centuries
He was a painter during the Renaissance.

Richter Scale
(rĭk′-tər skāl)

a scale for measuring earthquakes, with each step about ten times greater than the preceding one
It measured 5.9 on the Richter Scale.

rubbish
(rŭb′-ĭsh)

any material thrown away; trash
The dumpster is filled with rubbish.

sabotage
(săb′-ə-täzh)

deliberate destruction of bridges, railroads, etc., by enemies
Blowing up the train was an act of sabotage.

sacrifice
(săk′-rə-fīs)

giving up one thing for the sake of another
She made many sacrifices to send her children to college.

scene
(sēn)

the place where an event occurs
He went to the scene of the crime.

sequence
(sē′-kwəns)

the coming of one thing after another
Please tell me what happened in sequence.

short circuit
(shôrt sur′-kĭt)

a disrupted electrical flow
The lights went out because of a short circuit.

smelter
(smĕlt′-ər)

a place for refining metal
A lot of smoke came out of the smelter chimneys.

spillway
(spĭl-wā)

a channel to carry off excess water
Fifty thousand gallons of water pour over the spillway every day.

stricken
(strĭk'-ən)

to come down with an illness or pain
Last year I was stricken with the flu.

sturdy
(stʉr'-dē)

strong; firm
He was a sturdy little lad.

sue
(sōō)

to prosecute in a court in seeking justice, damages, etc.
He is being sued for a million dollars.

system
(sĭs'-təm)

an orderly method or plan
He has a fine bookkeeping system.

topsoil
(täp'-soil)

upper layer of soil
The wind blew the topsoil away.

tributary
(trĭb'-yî-těr-ē)

flowing into a larger one
That creek is a tributary of the Ohio River.

troposphere
(trō'-pō-sfîr)

lowest layer of the atmosphere (10 miles high)
A test question was about the troposphere.

twine
(twīn)

strong string or thread
Tie up that package with twine.

unthinkable
(ŭn-thĭnk-ə-bəl)

impossible; not to be considered or thought of
Dropping out of school is unthinkable.

vehicle
(vē'-ə-kəl)

any device for carrying persons or objects
Licenses are obtained from the Department of Motor Vehicles.

visibility
(vĭz-ə-bĭl-ə-tē)
the possibility of being seen; prevailing conditions of light, distance, etc.
Visibility for flying is very poor tonight.

vital
(vīt′-l)
essential to life; full of life; energetic
They tested all of his vital signs.